Animal Families

A young zebra crowds close to its mother at a water hole.

by Gene S. Stuart

BOOKS FOR YOUNG EXPLORERS
NATIONAL GEOGRAPHIC SOCIETY

Honk, honk! Here we come! A family of Canada geese
goes paddling by. The father leads the way.
Five fluffy goslings and the mother follow along.

Canada geese, like many other animals, mate for life.
The parents hatch eggs and raise chicks each year.
They lead their young to food and protect them.

A young dik-dik nibbles while its parents watch for danger. Dik-diks are tiny antelopes. Can you tell which is the father? He has horns on his head.

Back from hunting, a male robin brings food to his mate. She has carefully guarded their nest of chicks. Not all young animals live with both of their parents. Some live in other family groups. Each kind of animal forms a family group that suits it best.

Polar bears snuggle close in their Arctic home. Mother's big, fuzzy paws make soft, warm pillows for her cubs. In autumn, a female digs a cozy den beneath the snow.

6

The cubs are born there during the cold winter. They stay safe in the den until springtime comes. In this kind of animal family, a mother raises her babies alone.

Scrub-a-dub. A white-tailed deer cleans her baby with her tongue. Mother deer are called does, and the babies are called fawns. A fawn's spotted coat helps it hide. It lies very still in leafy shadows when the doe goes out alone to look for food.

What has a long, bumpy back and a long, toothy mouth? An alligator! Females build big nests in secret places. There they lay eggs. And there the young hatch. These three-week-old alligators go for a ride on their mother's back. Do you see two babies?

In some animal families, only the father takes care of
the young. Male emus sit on the nest until the eggs hatch.
Emus are about as tall as humans. Even though they are
birds, they do not fly. This emu watches as his chicks eat.

Under the sea, a male sea horse hangs onto a leaf with his
tail. A female has laid eggs in his pouch. After the eggs hatch,
tiny sea horses come out of the pouch and swim away.

Follow the leader! Arctic wolf pups trot behind an adult. Wolves live in large family groups called packs.

Peek-a-boo! A pup sees you! Older brothers and sisters help baby-sit the frisky pups. Parents and young wolves chase a younger pup. Play teaches pups how pack members behave.

Northern fur seal families have many females and only one male adult. The male is the largest. Do you see him?

A thirsty elephant family goes to a water hole to drink. Elephants are the largest animals that live on land. Several adult females and their young live together.

In elephant families, the females are usually related.
They help each other take care of the calves.
The oldest female is often the family leader.

Two lions watch for danger while others drink. A lion family is called a pride. It has females and their sons and daughters. One female is the family leader.

Tall giraffes must bend way down for water. Several females and their young live together.

riends together can be a family. Male impalas watch out for enemies. Sometimes many male and female impalas live together. At other times, the males form separate groups.

These young male bighorn sheep formed a group when they were two or three years old.

Capybaras live on land, but they like the water. They swim to find tasty water plants or to escape from enemies. One family may have 75 members.

Howler monkeys like to hang around in groups called troops. They howl to protect their area. Monkeys in a troop are not always related to one another. They live together because they are the same kind of animal.

D anger! An enemy is near—maybe a wolf! Males and
females in a musk-ox group quickly form a circle.
Very young calves stay inside the circle to be safe.

Musk-oxen live in the far north. Long, shaggy coats keep them warm in ice and snow. Males, females, and calves live together in large family groups called herds.

Moving on, white-fronted geese fly south for the winter. Many animal families change the places where they live as the seasons change.

Splash! A herd of wildebeests plunges into a stream. The animals are migrating. They are going to live in another area, where food will be easier to find.

Imagine a family this big! Hundreds of seabirds called gannets are nesting in one group on the shore. A group this large is called a colony. The colony is crowded, but each pair of gannets has its own nest.

Other gannets may come too close. If they do, parents defend their eggs and chicks. When the chicks have grown, all the birds in the colony go to sea for the winter. They stay in small groups until the next nesting time.

In the warm sun, prairie dogs munch, touch, and
nuzzle. Their colony shares an underground town.
Whether they have big families or small ones,
all animals live in ways that are best for their group.

Spotted dolphins live in families called schools. One school may have as many as 30 dolphins.

COVER: Gannets in a family clean one another. The male grooms the female. She tends their fluffy chick.

Published by

The National Geographic Society, Washington, D.C.
Gilbert M. Grosvenor, *President
and Chairman of the Board*
Melvin M. Payne, Thomas W. McKnew,
Chairmen Emeritus
Owen R. Anderson, *Executive Vice President*
Robert L. Breeden, *Senior Vice President,
Publications and Educational Media*

Prepared by

The Special Publications and School Services Division
Donald J. Crump, *Director*
Philip B. Silcott, *Associate Director*
Bonnie S. Lawrence, *Assistant Director*

Staff for this book

Jane H. Buxton, *Managing Editor*
John G. Agnone, *Illustrations Editor*
Viviane Y. Silverman, *Art Director*
Rebecca Lescaze, *Researcher*
Sharon Kocsis Berry, *Illustrations Assistant*
Carol R. Curtis, Marisa J. Farabelli, Lisa A. LaFuria,
Sandra F. Lotterman, Dru McLoud Stancampiano,
Marilyn Williams, *Staff Assistants*

Engraving, Printing, and Product Manufacture

George V. White, *Director,* and Vincent P. Ryan,
Manager, Manufacturing and Quality Management
David V. Showers, *Production Manager*
Lewis R. Bassford, *Production Project Manager*

Consultants

Dr. James M. Dietz, University of Maryland;
Craig Phillips, Biologist; Dr. George E. Watson,
St. Albans School, Washington, D.C.,
Scientific Consultants
Susan Altemus, *Educational Consultant*
Dr. Lynda Bush, *Reading Consultant*

Illustrations Credits

Anthony Bannister/ANTHONY BANNISTER LIBRARY (cover); Carol Hughes/BRUCE COLEMAN LTD. (1); Wayne Lankinen (2–3); D & R Sullivan/BRUCE COLEMAN LTD. (4); E. R. Degginger/BRUCE COLEMAN INC. (5); Joe McDonald/BRUCE COLEMAN INC. (6–7); Leonard Lee Rue III (8–9); Tim Thompson (9 right); ANIMALS ANIMALS/David C. Fritts (10); Jen & Des Bartlett (11, 18–19); Jim Brandenburg (12, 13 both); Erwin & Peggy Bauer/BRUCE COLEMAN INC. (14–15); Clem Haagner/ANTHONY BANNISTER LIBRARY (16–17); Robert Caputo (19 right); Frans Lanting/MINDEN PICTURES (20 left); ©Tom & Pat Leeson (20–21); Sven-Olof Lindblad/PHOTO RESEARCHERS, INC. (22); Sullivan & Rogers/BRUCE COLEMAN INC. (23); Erwin and Peggy Bauer (24–25, 30–31); Bates Littlehales (26 upper left); ANIMALS ANIMALS/Anup & Manoj Shah (26–27); Joe & Carol McDonald/BRUCE COLEMAN INC. (28–29); Roger Wilmshurst/BRUCE COLEMAN LTD. (29 right); Bill Curtsinger/PHOTO RESEARCHERS, INC. (32).

Library of Congress CIP Data
Stuart, Gene S.
  Animal families.

  (Books for young explorers)
  Summary: Text and pictures present families of different kinds of animals doing their ordinary activities.
  1. Familial behavior in animals—Juvenile literature. 2. Animals—Juvenile literature. [1. Familial behavior in animals. 2. Animals]
  I. Title. II. Series.
QL761.5.S78   1990   599'.056   90-5891
ISBN 0-87044-819-6 (regular edition)
ISBN 0-87044-824-2 (library edition)

After a snowstorm, whooper swans huddle for warmth. The swans raise their young in pairs. They fly south to winter homes at the end of the breeding season. There, hundreds often live together in one flock.

MORE ABOUT Animal Families

Some animals live alone for much of their lives. Many live in small families. Others gather at certain times, such as the breeding season, to be with thousands of their kind. The different ways of life that animals develop help ensure the survival, well-being, and reproduction of their kind. In this book, each major kind of animal family is marked with a different color block. Matching color blocks in this section point out more information on the natural history of animals in these groups.

The basic family *pages 2–5, 32*

A male and female may stay together during one breeding season or for many seasons. The two parents raise their young together; both share in the feeding, protecting, and teaching. Each family usually has its own territory, and the parents are about the same size. After their offspring leave to live on their own, parents may separate until the next breeding season. Many birds, such as Canada geese and robins, form this basic, or nuclear, family.

FRANS LANTING/MINDEN PICTURES

Monarch butterflies cover a tree trunk at their winter home in Mexico. In spring, monarchs may migrate as far as 2,000 miles to the United States and Canada.

Mothers raise offspring *pages 6–9*

After breeding, some male animals play no role in raising their offspring. The female takes full responsibility. Some make dens or nests. Polar bears and deer are two kinds of mothers that feed, defend, and teach their young alone.

Fathers raise offspring *pages 10–11*

Less common than females raising the young are male animals raising children with little or no female help. With some birds, such as emus, the mother lays eggs in a nest, but the father incubates the eggs and cares for the chicks.

Generations together *pages 12–13*

Animal grandparents, aunts, uncles, and cousins may live with a basic family. Usually there is only one breeding pair. Older offspring may still live with these parents when new offspring are born. Wolves belong to such extended families. All help care for the young. This gives older children necessary experience in being parents.

A male and his females *pages 14–15*

A single male, such as a northern fur seal, may have several mates during the breeding season. He defends his territory and protects his mates and their young. The group of females is called a harem.

Female leaders *pages 16–19*

Related females living together with their offspring may have an older female as their leader. She is often the mother of these females and the grandmother of the young. This animal family type is called a matriarchy. Elephants and lions live in matriarchies.

Male groups *pages 20–21*

When adult males leave home, they may be too young for a family of their own. Many, such as bighorn sheep, band into bachelor groups. Old males and non-breeding males also form bachelor groups.

Friends and relatives *pages 22–25, 32*

At times, some animals form large groups that may include nuclear families, extended families, and non-related members. These are called casual groups. They include herds and troops. Howler monkeys and capybaras form casual groups.

Changing homes *pages 26–27*

Animals of temperate climates may change homes, or migrate with the seasons. Some live in warm areas in winter and go to breeding areas in spring. Migratory animals, such as geese and monarch butterflies, can live in small families or in large casual groups.

Huge groups *pages 28–31*

At times, gannets or other animals form a group called a colony, with breeding areas near plentiful food. Their large numbers help protect them.

Additional Reading

Amazing Animal Groups. (Washington, D.C., National Geographic Society, 1981). Ages 4-8.

Animals Alone and Together: Their Solitary and Social Lives, by Margaret Cosgrove. (New York, Dodd, Mead & Co., 1978). Family reference.